# Inspire Your NEXT 30

*Journey Into the Light*

## Bridget Arrick
aka Author Vacation Girlfriend

# INSpire Your NEXT 30
# Journey Into the Light

By: Bridget Arrick aka Author Vacation Girlfriend

**INSpire Your NEXT 30
Journey Into the Light**

© 2025 Bridget Arrick aka Vacation Girlfriend

**All rights reserved.**

No part of this publication may be reproduced, distributed, or transmitted in any form or by any means, including photocopying, recording, or other electronic or mechanical methods, without the prior written permission of the author, except in the case of brief quotations embodied in critical reviews and certain other noncommercial uses permitted by copyright law.

For permission requests, contact the publisher at:
*authorvacationgirlfriend@gmail.com*
*Juiceobsession24@gmail.com*

Catalog-in-Publication Data is on file with the the Library of Congress

For permission requests, contact the publisher at:

*Published By : Author Vacation Girlfriend LLC, Harrington DE, 19952*

*Printed in the United States of America.*

**First Edition 2025**

*ISBN :979-8-9987170-5-5*

## Table of Contents

Day 1: ……………………..……….….. 1
Today Is The Day to Begin
Day 2: ……………………..……………. 2
Slow Down to Speed up
Day 3: ……………………..……........ 3
Drink Your Way to Clarity
Day 4: ……………………..……......... 4
Protect Your Peace
Day 5: …………………………………. 5
Move Your Body, Shift Your Mood
Day 6:…………………………………… 7
Honor your Temple
Day 7: ……………………………….. 8
Celebration and Reflection
Day 8 …………………………………… 9
Stay Focused, Stay Strong
Day 9: ……………………….………… 11
Release and Let Go
Day 10: ………………………………… 13
Now Fuel Your Fire
Day 11: ……………….………………. 15
Protect Your Energy
Day 12: …………….…………………. 16
Your Light Is Needed
Day 13: ……………….………………. 17
One Day Closer
Day 14: ……………….………………. 18
Celebration and Reflection!
Day 15: ……………........................ 19
Dance Into Your Breakthrough

Day 16: .................................................. 20
Speak It Into Existence
Day 17: .................................................. 21
Silence is Golden
Day 18: .................................................. 22
Move Your Body
Day 19: .................................................. 23
Tab Into Gratitude
Day 20 .................................................. 24
Release What No Longer Serves You
Day 21: .................................................. 25
Know Your own Strength
Day 22: .................................................. 26
Create Boundaries
Day 23: .................................................. 27
Dance Like Nobody's Watching
Day 24: .................................................. 28
 Release & Let Go
Day 25: .................................................. 29
 Speak Life
Day 26: .................................................. 30
Rest Is Resistance
Day 27: .................................................. 31
Choose Peace Over Chaos
Day 28: .................................................. 32
 Embrace Your Power
Day 29: .................................................. 33
Reflect and Replenish
Day 30: .................................................. 34
The Final Day - Cleansing & Breaking Soul Ties
Final Message ...................................... 36

# INSpire Your NEXT 30
# Journey Into the Light

## Dedication

*To every woman who's ever whispered, "There has to be more than this…"*

This is for you, Sis.

For the ones who kept pouring from an empty cup, who showed up tired but still sparkled, who prayed through tears and smiled through storms. This is for the late-night journalers, the early morning dreamers, the self-love warriors, and the queens who are finally putting themselves back at the top of their own to-do lists.

To the little girl inside of you who just wants to be seen, loved, and free this journey is your permission slip.

To my circle of sisterhood: the ones who hold space, speak truth, pour love, and bring light this book holds a piece of you in every page.

To the woman reading this right now: I see you. I honor your courage to start again. I celebrate your choice to grow, glow, and guard your peace like your life depends on it because, Sis, it does.

*You're not here by accident.
You didn't just stumble across this book.*

*You were divinely guided.*

So go ahead, hydrate that spirit, speak that life, dance into your breakthrough, and fall in love with you again.

So, Sis… are you ready? Let's go.

With love, laughter, and a whole lotta light,

**Bridget Arrick**
aka Author Vacation Girlfriend

### Today Is The Day to Begin
*"Ain't nothin' to it but to do it!"*

**African Proverb:** *"A journey of a thousand miles begins with a single step."*

**Bible Verse:** *"Behold, I will do a new thing; now it shall spring forth; shall ye not know it?" Isaiah 43:19*

**Meditation Moment**
Take a deep breath. Close your eyes and see yourself already walking out of your rut. Envision peace, success, and joy ahead of you. Inhale strength, exhale doubt. You got this.

**Mantra:** Today, I choose to begin.

**Hydration & Nutritional Moment**
Drink a tall glass of water to start your day. Add a slice of cucumber, lemon, or mint for a refreshing boost. This simple act is a physical step towards clearing your mind and body.

**Health Tip:** Hydrating first thing in the morning flushes toxins and kick-starts your energy. Make this a daily ritual.

**Reflection**
Write down one thing you're grateful for and one thing you want to change in the next 30 days. Today is your **Day 1.** Trust the process.

# Day 2: Slow Down to Speed Up

"You can't rush greatness, baby.!"

African Proverb: *"Patience can cook a stone."*

Bible Verse: *"Be still, and know that I am God."*
— Psalm 46:10

## Meditation Moment

Today, practice slowing down. Sit still for five minutes and breathe slowly. Feel your body relax. Allow your mind to slow down and reset. Time is not running out— you are right on time.

**Health Tip:** Warm lemon water helps balance your pH and energizes your phy naturally.

**Reflection** Write down one thing you often rush through in life. How can you intentionally slow down in that area? Reflect on the beauty of patience.

**Day 3:**

## Drink Your Way to Clarity
"Stay hydrated, stay winning!"

**African Proverb:** "Water has no enemy."

**Bible Verse:** *"But whoever drinks of the water that I shall give him will never thirst."* — John 4:14

### Meditation Moment
Visualize pure, clear water flowing through you, washing away stress, doubt, and heaviness. Picture yourself feeling light and refreshed. Take a few deep breaths and repeat:

**Mantra:** I am clear, I am focused, I am refreshed.

### Hydration & Nutritional Moment
Commit to drinking at least half your body weight in ounces of water today. Add fresh fruit like strawberries, lemon, or mint for flavor. Track your water intake and notice how you feel.

**Health Tip:** Proper hydration boosts energy, mental clarity, and digestion. Keep a water bottle with you all day.

### Reflection
How did you feel after prioritizing hydration today? Write down any changes in your mood, energy, or clarity.

**Day 4:**

## Protect Your Peace
"Protect your peace at all costs."

**African Proverb:** "Do not let the behavior of others destroy your inner peace."

**Bible Verse:** *"Peace I leave with you; my peace I give you."* — John 14:27

**Meditation Moment**
Close your eyes and visualize a protective bubble around you. Picture peace and light within the bubble, while negativity bounces off of it. Repeat:

**Mantra:** I protect my peace and energy.

**Hydration & Nutritional Moment**
Today, incorporate foods that promote peace and calm like blueberries, chamomile tea, and leafy greens. Avoid heavy or processed foods that may cloud your mood.

**Health Tip:** Eating light and clean supports mental clarity and inner peace.

**Reflection**
Write down one boundary you need to set to protect your peace. Commit to enforcing it today.

**Day 5:**

## Move Your Body, Shift Your Mood
*"Shake off that funk!"*

**African Proverb:** *"Movement is medicine."*

**Bible Verse:** *"A joyful heart is good medicine."* — *Proverbs 17:22*

**Meditation Moment**
Stand up, stretch, and move your body. Put on your favorite music and dance or do light exercise for 10 minutes. Notice the shift in your mood and energy.

**Mantra:** I move my body to move my mood.

**Hydration & Nutritional Moment**
Replenish your body with coconut water, watermelon juice, or a light fruit smoothie post-movement.

**Health Tip:** Moving your body daily releases stress and boosts happiness.

**Reflection**
Write down how you felt before and after moving your body. Did your mood shift?

**Smoothie Recipe for Glowing Skin (Day 5)**

**Radiant Skin Smoothie:**
1 cup watermelon chunks (hydrates skin)
1 cup pineapple (brightens skin)
1 handful of spinach (detoxes skin)
1/2 cucumber (hydrates)
1 cup coconut water
Ice as needed
Blend and enjoy. This smoothie will hydrate and give your skin a natural glow.

**Skincare Tip:** Apply aloe vera gel on your face at night. It promotes clear and even skin tone for melanin-rich skin.

# Day 6: Honor Your Temple

*"You carry your soul in you—treat it like home"*

**African Proverb:**
"He who has health has hope."

**Bible Verse**
" Know ye not that your body is a temple of the Holy Spirit which is in you, which ye have from God? —
1 Corinthians 6:19

**Mantra:**
My body is sacred. My body is strong. My body is mine.

**Hydration & Nutritional Moment**
Start your day with warm lemon water followed by a nourishing green juice, Fuel yourself with kale, avocado, berries and chia seeds.

**Reflection**
What part of your body do you need to treat with more love? Write down three ways you can honor your body today, whether rest, movement or nutrition.

**Health Tip:** *Nourish your body with natural oils and soak up enough sunlight for that essential dose of Vitamin D. Nature is your best friend. It heals the body and nurtures the soul.*

**Day 7:**

## Celebration and Reflection

Congratulations! You've made it through your first 7 days. Take a moment to celebrate but not too much that you don't continue.

**Reflection Prompt:** What has changed for you in the last 7 days? Write it down. If you missed a day, forgive yourself and keep going.

**Motivation:** Be your biggest cheerleader this week. Restart if necessary, but do not quit.

**Mantra:** I celebrate my progress and keep moving.

**Self care Tip:** "Celebrate through reflection. Run a warm bath, ground yourself in the moment, and take time to honor how far you've come. Prepare your spirit this next part of the journey is calling."

**Day 8:**

## Stay Focused, Stay Strong
"Ain't no no stopping me now!"

**African Proverb:** "However long the night, the dawn will break."

**Bible Verse:** *"I can do all things through Christ who strengthens me."* — Philippians 4:13

**Meditation Moment**
Sit in silence for five minutes. Picture yourself crossing the finish line of your 30-day journey. Feel the pride, the joy, the strength. Let that vision fuel you today.

**Mantra:** I am unstoppable. I am focused. I am finishing strong.

**Hydration & Nutritional Moment**
Drink a green smoothie packed with spinach, cucumber, pineapple, and ginger. This will boost your energy and cleanse your body.

**Health Tip:** Start your day with green juice to detox your body and clear your skin.

**Smoothie Recipe for Energy (Day 8)**

**Green Energy Smoothie:**
1 cup spinach
1/2 cucumber
1 cup pineapple
1 small piece of ginger
1 cup coconut water
Ice as needed
Blend and enjoy for a natural energy boost.

**Skincare Tip:** Apply rose water to your face after cleansing. It hydrates and balances your skin.

**Reflection**
What is one thing you want to leave behind after these 30 days? Write it down.

**Day 9:**

## Release and Let Go
*"You can't carry old baggage into your new life."*

**African Proverb:** *"When the music changes, so does the dance."*

**Bible Verse:** *"Cast all your anxiety on Him because He cares for you." — 1 Peter 5:7*

### Meditation Moment
Sit quietly and think about something heavy you've been carrying — a grudge, worry, or fear. Imagine placing it in a box, closing it, and handing it over to God. Breathe and feel lighter.

**Mantra:** I release what no longer serves me.

### Hydration & Nutritional Moment
Drink warm tea today (like chamomile or ginger tea) to promote relaxation and calm. Avoid heavy or processed foods.

**Health Tip:** Drinking herbal tea helps reduce anxiety and promotes peace.

### Reflection
Write down one thing you need to release emotionally or mentally.

**Spiritual Release Ritual**
Write down everything you're ready to release fears, doubts, pain and place it into a burning bowl. As the flames rise, let it symbolize your readiness to step into the next chapter of your journey. Once cooled, respectfully scatter the ashes outdoors as an offering to your ancestors. Honor their wisdom and protection as you move forward.

**Remember:** safety first.
Now take a deep breath… doesn't that feel lighter?
 Spiritual release

**Day 10:**

## Now Fuel Your Fire
*"Get yo' fire back!"*

**African Proverb:** "If you want to go fast, go alone. If you want to go far, go together."

**Bible Verse:** *"For the Spirit God gave us does not make us timid, but gives us power, love and self-discipline." — 2 Timothy 1:7*

### Meditation Moment
Sit quietly and recall a time when you felt powerful and unstoppable. Channel that energy back into yourself today.

**Mantra:** My fire is alive. My passion is strong. I am capable.

### Hydration & Nutritional Moment
Drink a protein smoothie after a light workout or brisk walk today to re-energize your body.

### Smoothie Recipe for Strength (Day 10):
1 cup almond milk
1 banana
1 tablespoon almond butter
1 scoop protein powder
Ice as needed
*Blend and drink after moving your body.*

**Skincare Tip:** Apply a honey mask to your face for 10 minutes to brighten and soften your skin.

**Reflection**
Write down one thing you're passionate about and how you can pursue it more actively.

# DAY 11: PROTECT YOUR ENERGY
## PROTECT YOUR VIBE.

*African Proverb:* He who knows how to keep quiet keeps his friends."

Bible Verse: "Above all else, guard your heart, for everything you do flows from it."
— Proverbs 4;23

### MEDITATION MOMENT
Close your eyes and imagine a protective shield around you. Negative energy cannot penetrate it. You are covered in peace.

**Mantra: I protect my energy and guard my peace.**

### HYDRATION & NUTRITIONAL MOMENT
Drink cucumber-mint water today for a refreshing detox.

**HEALTH TIP:** Cucumber-mint water helps reduce bloating and hydrates your skin.

### REFLECTION
Write down one boundary you will enforce to protect your energy.

## Day 12:

### Your Light Is Needed
"Shine, baby, shine!"

**African Proverb:** "The sun does not forget a village just because it is small."

**Bible Verse:** *"You are the light of the world. A city on a hill cannot be hidden."* Matthew 5:14

### Meditation Moment
Visualize your inner light shining bright, touching everyone around you. Picture yourself walking with confidence and joy.

**Mantra:** My light is powerful and needed in this world.

### Hydration & Nutritional Moment
Drink a tropical fruit smoothie to boost your energy and glow.

### Smoothie Recipe for Glow (Day 12):
1 cup mango
1 cup pineapple
1 cup coconut water
Ice as needed
Blend and enjoy.

**Skincare Tip:** Apply vitamin C serum to brighten your skin and fade dark spots.

### Reflection
Write down one way you can spread light and positivity today..

# Day 13: One Day Closer

*"We ain't done yet!"*

**African Proverb:**
*"Little by little, the bird builds its nest."*

**Bible Verse:**
*"Being confident of this, that he who began a good work in cou will carry it on to completion."*
Philippians 1:6

**Meditation Moment**
Focus on progress, not perfection

**Hydration & Nutritional Moment**
Drink lemon-infused water and eat a colorful fruit salad today.

**Health Tip:** The more color in your food, the more nutrients you consume.

**Mantra:**
I am one step closer to my best self.

**Reflection**
Write down one thing you've accomplished since Day 1.

## Day 14:

### Celebration and Reflection!

Congratulations you've completed 14 days! Pause and reflect. Forgive yourself for any missed days. Celebrate how far you've come.

**Reflection Prompt**: What changes have you seen in yourself or your routine? Write it down.

**Motivation**: You've started strong, now finish even stronger.

**Mantra**: I am proud of my progress.

**Make today a Self Care Day!**

**Self Care:** Give yourself permission to slow down and pour back into you. Take the time to nurture and detox your body whether through a rejuvenating steam session, a soul-soothing massage, or simply quiet rest. You deserve this moment of peace, healing, and renewal. 🧖🏾‍♀️🕊️✨

**Now let's continue this journey, we are halfway there !**

# Day 15: Dance Into Your Breakthrough

*Move like you already won.*

**African Proverb:**
"When the rhythm of the drum changes, the dance must also change."

**Bible Verse:**
"Let them praise his name with dancing."
Psalm 149:3

**Meditation Moment**
Play your favorite feel good song. Close your eyes, let your body move freely, and dance like you're already celebrating your success.

**Mantra:** I dance in joy, knowing my breakthroug is here.

**Smoothie Recipe for Joy (Day 15):**
1 cup strawberries - 1 cup almond milk
1 cup almond milk - Ice as needed
Blend and dance while you drink it

**Skincare Tip**
After your dance, rinse your face with cool water to refresh your skin.

**Reflection**
Write down how you felt after dancing. Did your mood shift?

**Day 16:**

## Speak It Into Existence
"Speak what you seek until you see what you said."

**African Proverb:** "The tongue has no bones but is strong enough to break a heart."

**Bible Verse:** *"Death and life are in the power of the tongue."* — *Proverbs 18:21*

### Meditation Moment
Stand in front of a mirror and declare positive affirmations about your life. Speak them until you feel their truth.

**Mantra:** I speak life, success, and abundance over myself.

### Hydration & Nutritional Moment
Drink citrus-infused water today (like lemon, lime, and orange).

**Health Tip:** Citrus water boosts your immune system and clears your skin.

### Reflection
Write down 3 positive things you will manifest in your life. Work on those items for the next 30 days.

# Day 17: Silence Is Golden

*"If it costs you your peace, it's too expensive."*

**African Proverb**
Silence is also speech.

**Bible Verse**
"The Lord gives strength to his people; the Lord blesses his people with peace."
Psalm 29:11

**Meditation Moment**
Visualize yourself in a peaceful, calm place. Imagine peace filling your body and mind.

**Mantra**
Peace surrounds me.
Peace lives within me.

**Hydration & Nutritional Moment**
Drink chamomile or lavender tea today to calm your spirit.

**Health Tip:** Drinking calming tea before bed improves sleep and reduces stress.

**Reflection** Write down one thing you will no longer allow to disturb your peace.

**Day 18:**

## Move Your Body
"Your body is your temple, keep it strong."

**African Proverb:** "He who has health has hope; and he who has hope has everything."

**Bible Verse:** *"Do you not know that your body is a temple of the Holy Spirit?" 1 Corinthians 6:19*

### Meditation Moment
Go for a brisk walk, do yoga, or dance. Move your body and feel your strength.

**Mantra:** My body is powerful, strong, and healthy.

### Hydration & Nutritional Moment
Drink coconut water today to replenish electrolytes after moving your body.

**Health Tip:** Staying hydrated after physical activity keeps your energy high.

### Reflection
Write down how you felt after moving your body. Did I release any stress anxiety? Did you feel stronger?

**Day 19:**

## Tap Into Gratitude
*"Gratitude turns what you have into enough."*

**African Proverb:** *"Give thanks for a little and you will find a lot."*

**Bible Verse:** *"Give thanks in all circumstances."* 1 Thessalonians 5:18

### Meditation Moment
Write down 10 things you are grateful for today. Feel the gratitude as you write.

**Mantra:** Gratitude opens the door to abundance.

### Hydration & Nutritional Moment
Drink warm lemon water with honey today to boost your immune system.

**Health Tip:** Warm lemon water aids digestion and improves skin glow.

### Reflection
Gratitude is more than a feeling, it's a spiritual law. It softens the heart, opens doors to new blessings, and keeps your soul grounded in humility. Even the hard moments carry hidden gifts when you choose to see them.
Remember: What you honor grows. Gratitude is the light that makes room for even more to be thankful for.

Write down 3 unexpected blessings you've received in the last 30 days. ✨ 🙍🏾‍♀️🕊️ ✨

# Day 20: Release What No Longer Serves You

*"Let that go. It's not yours to carry."*

**African Proverb:**
*"When the music changes, so does the dance."*

**Bible Verse:**
*"Cast all your anxiety on him because he cares for you."* — 1 Peter 5:7

**Meditation Moment**
Write down three things or people you need to release emotionally. Close your eyes and imagine yourself setting them free.
**Mantra:** I release what no longer serves me. I am free.

**I release** what no longer serves me. I am free.

**Reflection**
Write a goodbye letter to what you are releasing. Burn it or tear it as a sign of release.

**Hydration & Nutritional Moment:**
Soul Cleansing Smoothie:
1 cup pinespple
1 cup coconut water
½ lime (juiced)
Handful of mint leaves
Ice
Blend and sip while visualizing peace.

# DAY 21: Celebrate Your Strength

'You didn't come this far to only come this far."

### African Proverb:
The brave man is not he who does not feel afraid, but he who conquers that fear.

### Bible Verse 4.3
I can do all things through Christ who strengthens me.

### Meditation Moment
Stand tall, arms outstretched, and say:
I am strong. I am powerful. I am resilient.

### Hydration & Nutritional Moment
Warrior Smoothie
- 1 cup kale or spinach
- 1 green apple
- 1/2 lemon (juiced)
- 1 cup water or coconut water

### Reflection
Write about a time when you were strong, even when you didn't feel like it

# Day 22:

## Create Boundaries
"Not everyone deserves access to you."

**African Proverb:** *"Do not look where you fell but where you slipped."*

**Bible Verse:** *"Above all else, guard your heart, for everything you do flows from it."* Proverbs 4:23

**Meditation Moment:** Close your eyes and visualize a protective bubble around you, blocking out negative energy.

**Mantra:** My energy is sacred. I protect it at all costs.

**Hydration & Nutritional Moment :** Energy Shield Tea: Hot water Fresh ginger (sliced) Lemon Honey Drink while setting intentions for protection.

**Reflection:**
"Creating boundaries is an act of self-love. It's how you teach others to honor your time, energy, and peace. Protect your light set the standard."
Write down people or environments that drain your energy.

# DAY 23:
# Dance Like No One's Watching

*"Shake it off."*

African Proverb: "When the drumbeat changes, the dancers must also change."

— Psalm 30:11

### Meditation Moment

Turn on your favorite song and dance freely for 15 minutes.

*Mantra;* Joy flows through me.

### Reflection

Write about how you felt after dancing.

**Day 24:**

## Release & Let Go
"Drop that dead weight."

**African Proverb:** *"When the roots run deep, the wind can't shake you."*

**Bible Verse:** *"Cast all your anxiety on Him because He cares for you."* — 1 Peter 5:7

### Meditation Moment
Take five deep breaths. With every exhale, let the stress slide right off you.

**Mantra:** I'm done holding what's not mine.

### Hydration & Nutritional Moment

**Detox Water:**
Cucumber slices

Lemon wedges

Mint leaves

Cold water

**Sip while saying goodbye to the heaviness.**

### Reflection
Who or what are you finally ready to let go of? Write it down and release it.

**Day 25:**

## Speak Life
"Talk that talk but make it love."

**African Proverb:** "The tongue don't weigh much, but it's heavy when used wrong."

**Bible Verse:** *"Death and life are in the power of the tongue."* Proverbs 18:21

**Meditation Moment**
Say three affirmations out loud that gas you up.

**Mantra:** My words spark light. I speak power.
Hydration & Nutritional Moment

**Uplift Smoothie:**
1 banana

1/2 cup blueberries

1/2 cup oat milk

1 tablespoon flaxseed

*Drink like a champ. Talk like a healer*.
**Reflection**
What's the most powerful thing you've ever told yourself? Say it again.

**Day 26:**

## Rest Is Resistance
"Rest ain't lazy it's legendary."

**African Proverb:** "A man who flexes first, skips the wisdom."

**Bible Verse:** *"Come to me, all you who are weary and burdened, and I will give you rest."* Matthew 11:28

**Meditation Moment**
Lay back. Breathe deep. Let your mind float.

**Mantra:** My rest is revolutionary.

**Hydration & Nutritional Moment**

**Calm Tonic:**
Warm water

Chamomile tea

Lemon

Drizzle of honey

*Sip slow. Let the peace pour in.*

**Reflection**
Self care Tip: "Celebrate through reflection. Run a warm bath, ground yourself in the moment, and take time to honor how far you've come. Prepare your spirit this next part of the journey is calling."
When's the last time you gave yourself permission to just be?

**Day 27:**

## Choose Peace Over Chaos
*"Don't match energy. Protect yours."*

**African Proverb:** *"If your soul is calm, nothing outside can shake you."*

**Bible Verse:** *"Blessed are the peacemakers, for they will be called children of God." Matthew 5:9*

**Meditation Moment**
Imagine yourself floating down a calm river. No noise, no drama, just flow.

**Mantra:** I guard my peace like treasure.

**Hydration & Nutritional Moment**

**Peaceful Infusion:**
Lavender or chamomile tea

Lemon slice

Basil leaf

*Sip in silence.*

**Reflection**
What situations knock you off balance? How can you stay rooted next time?

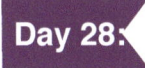

**Day 28:**

### Embrace Your Power
"Own it. Don't shrink."

**African Proverb:** "Wisdom's too big for one set of arms so stop playing small."

**Bible Verse:** *"God has not given us a spirit of fear, but of power, love, and a sound mind."* 2 Timothy 1:7

**Meditation Moment**
Look at yourself in the mirror and say: "I'm built for this."

**Mantra:** I'm not backing down, I'm rising.
**Hydration & Nutritional Moment**
 Power Boost Juice:
1 orange

1/2 beet

1/2 carrot

Dash of turmeric

*Drink like the force you are.*

**Reflection**
What part of you are you finally ready to stop hiding?

# Day 29
# Reflect & Replenish
*Look back—but don't stay there.*

**African Proverb:** "Wisdom don't show up overnight.

**Bible Verse:** "Examine yourselves… test yourselves

**Meditation Moment**
Breathe. Reflect. Realize how far you've come,

**Mantra:** *I've grown through what I've gone through.*

**Hydration & Nutritional Moment**

Reflection Salad:
- Mixed greens
- Cherry tomatoes
- Avocado
- Cucumber
- Olive oil & lemon drizzle

**Hydration:** 1 liter of water with mint & lime

Nourish yourself, You earned this

**Reflection**
What did this journey teach you about you?
Write your truth. Honor your light

## The Final Day - Cleansing & Breaking Soul Ties
"Close the door so new ones can open."

**African Proverb:** "The axe forgets, but the tree remembers."

**Bible Verse:** *"Behold, I make all things new."* Revelation 21:5

### Meditation Moment
Light a white candle. Write down any remaining emotional, spiritual, or mental ties you have. Then, speak out loud:
I break all ties that no longer serve me. I am free. I am whole. I am renewed.
Burn the paper as a symbolic release.

### Hydration & Nutritional Moment
### Cleansing Juice:
1 cup soursop
1 cup coconut water
1/2 lime

*Drink and feel the cleansing energy.*

**Crystal Purchase Recommendation**

**Rose Quartz:** To remind yourself of self-love.
**Clear Quartz:** For clarity and healing.
**Obsidian:** To protect your energy moving forward.

Sage your home and area for a fresh energy cleanse

**Final Reflection**
Write a letter to your future self, filled with love, hope, and vision.

**Next Steps:**
Continue dancing, hydrating, and speaking life into yourself.
Surround yourself with positive, uplifting energy.
Protect your peace without guilt.

# Final Message To You

You did not stumble upon this journey by accident. The fact that you completed this 30-day inspiration journey means something powerful has shifted in you. Old energy has been removed, new light has entered, and you have unlocked the power to move forward without hesitation. Do not be afraid to release, rebuild, and reinvent yourself. You are divinely guided, loved, and protected: Keep choosing yourself daily, and never forget: you are worthy of a life filled with joy, peace, and abundance.

With love, light, and power — keep rising.

www.ingramcontent.com/pod-product-compliance
Lightning Source LLC
Chambersburg PA
CBHW042259090526
44582CB00005B/110